ANOTHER SPOT ON MY BUM

ANOTHER SPOT ON MY BUM

And Other Rude Poems

Gez Walsh

Scratching Shed Publishing Ltd

Copyright © Gez Walsh, 2011
All rights reserved
The moral right of the author has been asserted

First published by Scratching Shed Publishing Ltd in 2011
Registered in England & Wales No. 6588772.
Registered office:
47 Street Lane, Leeds, West Yorkshire. LS8 1AP

www.scratchingshedpublishing.co.uk

ISBN 978-956804303

No part of this book may be reproduced or transmitted in any form or by any other means without the written permission of the publisher, except by a reviewer who wishes to quote brief passages in connection with a review written for insertion in a magazine, newspaper or broadcast

Illustrations © Howard Priestley

A catalogue record for this book is available from the British Library.

Typeset in FS Ingrid Light and Chalkboard

Printed and bound in the United Kingdom by
L.P.P.S.Ltd, Wellingborough, Northants, NN8 3PJ

In memory of Peter Walsh
And Gordon Poulter
Two good men.

Acknowledgements

I would like to thank the people at Scratching Shed for their bacon sarnies and patience. I would also like to thank my buddy Elaine Duffy for her patience but no bacon sarnies.

I would also like to take this opportunity to thank Howard Priestley one of the finest undiscovered artistic talents in the country for his brilliant illustrations.

Last but not least I would like to thank my wife Carol and my son Lee for putting up with my charm, wit, genius and modesty!

Foreword
by William Shakespeare (Deceased)

Gadzooks! What is this parchment I hold before me? Why sire this has been scribed by a mind no greater than a pleb!

Surely to compare such a work with the beauty that my mind hath created is to do an injustice to the many scholars that have laughed and wept with my creations?

Please sire, remove this pile of dung from mine eyes so I may see clear once more!

William Shakespeare, Roundhay 2011

Frog head

The doctor was in his surgery
Trying to invent a cure,
When all of a sudden
There was a knock at the door.
The doctor shouted, "Enter!
Come and lay upon the bed."
When in walked a small boy
With a frog stuck to his head.
The doctor pulled at the frog
Then he had a close look:
It was growing from his head
So he looked in a book.
The doctor said, "It's amazing.
How did this start, son?"
The frog replied,
"As a spot on my bum."

The spot on my bum

Good grief! This spot on my bum,
I've squeezed it so much that my cheeks
Have gone numb.
It's big and it's red
With a big yellow top,
I've squeezed it with pliers,
But still it won't pop!
I've soaked it in water,
I've put on some cream.
Mum had a squeeze
Which just made me scream.
I can't sit down now,
The pain is quite dire,
My spot is glowing
And my bum is on fire!
I cried to my mum,
"Just one last try, please!"
So mum, with a grip like Superman,
Started to squeeze.
Yes, mum had hold of my spot
With a vice-like grip,
My eyes they were popping
And I was biting my lip.
My body started shaking without restraint,
My legs they wobbled,
I started to faint.
Then my mum cried out with such distaste
Because my spot, like a time-bomb,
Had exploded in her face!

All Things Fuzzbutt

All things bright and beautiful
All creatures great and small
Little Lord Fuzzbutt
Has shot and stuffed them all!

He sneaked up behind a rhino
Munching on some grass
He took out his big gun
And shot it up its behind so vast

All things bright and beautiful
All creatures great and small
Little Lord Fuzzbutt
Has shot and stuffed them all

Once he shot a crocodile
That wasn't very happy
It bit off old Fuzzbutt's hand
Because it was still alive and snappy
Fuzzbutt wasn't bothered
Too dim to feel the blues
He had the crocodile skinned
And turned into snappy new shoes

All things bright and beautiful
All creatures great and small
Little Lord Fuzzbutt
Has shot and stuffed them all

While out hunting tiger
In a jungle so remote
He thought he'd bagged one
But it was a helper in a stripy coat
The locals weren't too happy

They started to jeer and call
Because Fuzzbutt wanted to stuff him
And mount him on his wall

All things bright and beautiful
All creatures great and small
Little lord Fuzzbutt
Has shot and stuffed them all

While out in North America
Hunting bear out in a wood
The trapper shouted, "bear behind!"
Fuzzbutt said, "yes it looks so good!"

All things bright and beautiful
All creatures great and small
Little Lord Fuzzbutt
Has shot and stuffed them all

And on the fateful day
When Fuzzbutt upped and died
All the indigenous creatures
Drew a breath and sighed
They were all so happy
All of them so chuffed
The only regret they all had
Was that they couldn't have him stuffed!

All things bright and beautiful
All creatures great and small
Little Lord Fuzzbutt
Has shot and stuffed them all!

Someone's nicked my knickers

Someone's nicked my knickers
And I just want them back.
If I find out who's nicked them
I'll give them such a smack.

I left them in my top drawer
So they would be easy to find.
I can't go out 'til I find them –
Not with a bare behind!

I've looked in my wardrobe
From the bottom to the top,
I've looked behind my radiator
Where I found an old green sock.

Oh, who has nicked my knickers?
Just where could they have gone?
Wait! I've just remembered...
This morning, I put them on!

Dyslexia

I suffer from something called Dyslexia
So I find it hard to read and write.
It doesn't mean that I'm stupid,
In fact in some things I'm quite bright.

But I would really like to know,
So teachers please do tell,
Why you gave my problem such a name
Which most people can't spell?

Ealing Feeling

There was once a young man from Ealing
In his stomach he had a funny feeling.
He ate baked beans one night
Then gave himself a fright
When his fart pebble-dashed the ceiling

A Gift of Love

I loved a girl named Emma,
She really was quite nice.
I gave her my heart forever,
She gave me her head lice!

The Question

They said he wouldn't do it,
He didn't have the guts.
To ask her such a question,
Surely would be nuts!
But they hadn't counted on Dan,
They didn't have a hunch
That he dare say it,
And that he couldn't take a punch!
He walked straight up to her,
And looked her in the eyes.
But when she kicked him between the legs,
It was certainly a surprise!
They said he was rude,
And I certainly agree.
But he did have to spend a night,
In the local A&E
He sat there with all the drunks
From yobs to drunken yuppies
All because he asked Claire Griffin,
If she was fat or smuggling puppies!

Can I go to the toilet?

"Please miss, can I go to the toilet?"
"No, you should have gone at break time."

"Please miss, can I go to the toilet?
"No, just do your sums."

"Please miss, can I go to the toilet?
"No, you shouldn't have drunk so much."

"Please miss, CAN I GO TO THE TOILET?
"No, you will have to learn to control yourself."

"Please miss, er, can I change my trousers?

Smelt it!

When you're sitting in your own fog
Don't blame it on the dog!
He who smelt it
DEALT IT!

When you're sitting on a train
Smelling like a drain
He who smelt it
DEALT IT!

When you're sitting in your class
With a smell coming from your... Bum
He who smelt it
DEALT IT!

So if you're really smart
When you do a silent fart
Walk away and say
He who smelt it
DEALT IT!

Comput*rrs

CoMputers are GOO£d,
Computerrrs are bAd,
When they don't work
th"y drive me mˆd.

Who Am I?

I can empty a room
I'm never fun
When I'm around
People run

I can turn up at a bar b cue,
A party or dance
You can meet me anywhere
From Brisbane to France

I'm known in all countries
By many different names
But no matter what they call me
The outcome is always the same

I'm never, ever nice
People say that I'm rotten
When you meet me
The world falls out of your bottom!

Who am I?

Teenager

Now that my brother's a teenager
He has turned into a bore,
And now he's growing hairs
Where he didn't have them before.

He has lost the power of speech,
He now acts like a spoilt brat;
Mum says it's just a phase
And I'll end up like that.

His body is now changing,
His emotions are all in knots,
His voice goes up and down
And his face is covered in spots.

He says that we don't understand
And that we no longer care.
He says he's now a young man
With spots and fluffy facial hair.

He wants a place of his own,
Dad says it's just a dream
Because it's hard to get a house
When you're only thirteen!

Having A Bad Time?

My sister took a note
To her teacher today;
Excuse her from swimming
Is what it had to say.
Mum had written the note,
My sister was still in bed.
The note had stated
She was having a bad period.
This really got me angry;
My sister lay there grinning.
I've had lots of bad periods
But I didn't get off swimming!
Can you remember that time
My little hamster went and died?
For me that was a bad period,
I just sat and cried and cried.
Mum then tried to explain
That because I am a boy
I will never have a period,
And for that I should jump for joy.
But I think it's unfair,
I think it's so unjust.
I am going to start a campaign,
I think that I must.
Boys and girls are equal,
Right is on my side;
My sister's bad period is no worse
Than when my little hamster died.
So come on friends,
Make a lot of noise;
Fair play for everyone,
And bad periods for boys.

Elaine

There was once a young girl called Elaine
All the boys thought her insane
She would get funny looks
When she said she loved books
I think there's something wrong with her brain!

Bad Mouth

Helen has really black teeth,
Which causes her bad breath.
It smells like something in her mouth,
Has recently had a death.
She's really very pretty,
But if she were to yawn,
Birds would fall from the skies,
And litter your front lawn.
She once asked me,
If I fancied a kiss.
But I didn't have a gas mask,
So I said I'd give it a miss.
But she's going to the dentist,
And everything will be fine,
And if she's looking for a boyfriend,
I will be the first in line!

Fido's Foul Surprise

I can't go home tonight,
My dog has caused me grief.
If I were to meet my big brother
I would surely lose my teeth.

I can see why he's angry,
Yes, I too would be upset,
But I wasn't the one
That pooed in his crash helmet!

Mum said he's so angry
That his face is burning red
Because he didn't see it
Until he'd put it on his head!

Norah's Nasty Knickers

Norah had some knickers
That were not very good–
A witch gave them to her
While out walking in the wood.

Norah was usually a good girl
With an attitude so mild,
But when she wore the Knickers
She became a horrible little child.

The witch had cast a spell,
With lots of cackles and sniggers,
And turned a pair of ordinary pants
Into a pair of nasty knickers.

They make Norah swear,
And often started fights;
The knickers just laughed
Beneath Norah's school tights.

Norah's mum had noticed the change,
The moans and the bickers.
She said, "I've seen this magic before–
She's wearing nasty knickers!"

The knickers soon realised
Norah's mum was on their case
Therefore, they escaped from the wash basket
That night with great haste.

Norah then saw the knickers on TV
So she let out such a cry,
"That woman's wearing my nasty knickers."
As the woman said, "you are the weakest link, goodbye."

Shelly

There was once a young girl called Shelly
Who wanted to appear on the telly
She met Simon Cowell
And made him scowl
When she did a strange dance with her belly!

Never Kiss My Dog

Never kiss my dog
Whatever you do,
I've just seen him in the garden
Eating his own pooh!

Life's Great Mysteries

Why do boys think that farting is funny?

Why does bottled water cost so much money?

Why do girls paint their faces?

Why do men in flash cars wear red braces?

Who wears jeans with an elastic waist?

Who thinks broccoli is a nice taste?

Why do women wear shoes that could cripple?

And why on earth does a man need a nipple?

I Love Bullies

Bullies are cool,
Bullies are ace,
Bullies like to punch you
In the face.

They take your money
And rough you up
If you dare tell a teacher
And grass them up.

I love bullies,
They're so full of charm.
Now that I've written this
Will you stop breaking my arm?

Dorothy Trip

Dorothy Trip had such enormous lips
That they dragged along the floor.
She was in such a fix,
With her rubber lips
That once she caught them in a door.
So it's sad to say,
But with all the other kids she could not play,
Because her huge rubber lips always got in the way.
But one day, just by mistake,
Dorothy did something that the other kids thought was great.
While they were on a school outing,
Dorothy tripped over her lips,
Fell off a bridge and started shouting.
The other kids screamed, "Miss, just look at Trip,
She's bungee jumping with her lips!"
Teacher shouted, "Trip, you fool!"
But as Dorothy bounced up an down,
The kids said, "Cool!"
So now everyone is friends with Dorothy Trip,
The little girl with the amazing bungee jumping lips.

The Zip

I had to go to hospital
And I felt such a drip
'Cos this morning I rushed to get dressed
And caught my willy in my zip.

First my body went rigid
Then I let out such a shout:
I gave my willy a tug
But it wouldn't come back out.

So I shouted for my dad,
He started to laugh.
He said, "Let me try."
I replied, "No, you'll cut it in half!"

He then took me to the hospital
Where a nurse asked if I was sick.
I replied, "NO, I've just a sore willy."
Then she pulled my zip down so quick

I shot off that bed
And banged into the door
Screaming, "She's cut my willy off!"
Before fainting to the floor.

So all heed this warning,
It's a very good tip;
Don't rush to get dressed,
And watch out for that zip!

Little Tommy Hamster

Little Tommy hamster
Has gone up to the sky
I put him and his ball in the tumble drier
What a way to die!

My Name Is

Oh, I wish I was called Lynne,
Or Gemma or Lucy.
Any name would do,
I'm really not that choosy.

They could call me Charlotte,
Or Emma or Jane.
In fact they could call me anything,
Please just give me another name.

Yes, Mum could have named me
By lots of names,
From Kirsty to Annie,
But she went and amed me after Grandma,
She went and named me Fanny!

Who Weed on the Toilet Seat?

Every night at our house
My mum and sister bleat
To my brother, Dad and me:
"Who's weed on the toilet seat?"

They say, "Just lift the seat up!"
And that men and boys don't think.
I don't know why they're blaming me
Because I always wee in the sink!

Bad Teeth

There was on old man from Neath
Who had very bad yellow teeth,
But things soon improved
When he had then removed
By a very nice dentist called Keith.

Grandad in Space

Grandad nearly gave us all a heart attack,
The day he had a fart attack.
It all started one afternoon,
When a strange eggy smell filled the room.
We were all gasping for air by half past three,
But he just kept on farting,
Right through 'Neighbours' and while eating his tea.
That was it we could take no more,
We opened all the windows
And we opened all the doors.
I said, " It's no good Mum, we'll have to move him,
He's been eating baked beans.
There's no way to stop him now,
He's turned into a rampant farting machine."
So we all pushed Grandad outside in his wheel chair,
But his farts were now getting stronger,
They were now lifting him in the air.
So we all held him down,
To make sure he didn't take off,
But the smell was so bad,
That we started to splutter and cough.
But Grandad knew how to sort things out,
He took out his tobacco and filled his pipe,
Then got out his matches to set it alight.
My Dad shouted, "No don't strike that match!"
But it was too late, he did it,
And all we could do was stand back and watch.

The match ignited Grandad's fart,
With such a ferocious pace,
That it blew him out of his wheelchair
And deep into uncharted space.
A passing space shuttle saw him from their control room.
They said, "Mission control, we have a problem.

We've just seen an old man with a pipe,
Orbiting the moon."
Grandad saw the space shuttle, he waved at them.

"Hello!" he yelled, then he headed back for earth,
Still fart propelled.
He was soon through the atmosphere,
He was now all steamy and wet.
He turned his bum to the ground
And he hovered around, just like a harrier jump jet.
Grandad descended to earth,
With such elegance and grace,
His gas was running out,
But he still had a cheeky smile upon his face.
So that was it, his adventure was now over,
Although his wheelchair was now blown apart.
But I'm proud to have a Granddad
Who had travelled the galaxy,
Propelled by a fart.

To The Doctor's

I had to go to the doctor's
Because I wasn't feeling well.
Every time I pooped I poohed,
And my room began to smell.

The doctor said, "Come over here
And don't be frightened, son."
Then he asked me what the problem was,
I said it was my bum.

He said, "Just take these tablets,
And you'll soon be feeling fine."
I hope to heck that he is right
Cos I keep pooping all the time.

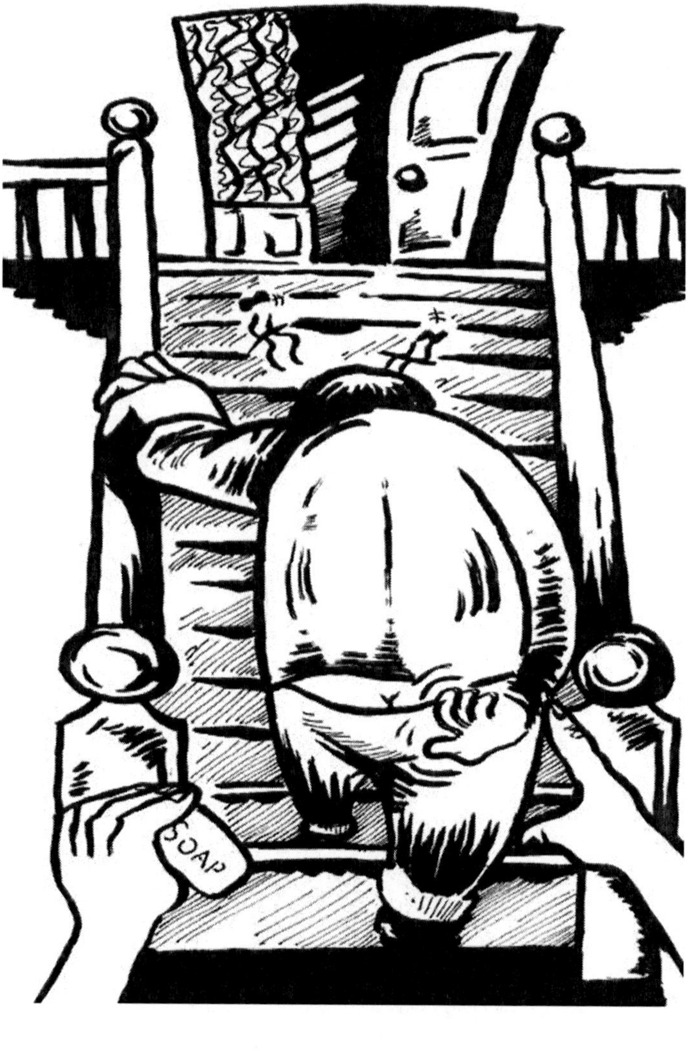
SOAP

Can't Wash

I think that you're starting to smell
You're making us all unwell
So loose that scowl
Go get a towel
And lots of smelly shower gel!

Mum I can't wash!
I can't wash myself
Get rid of the dirt
And it will be bad for my health

Even the dog has given up all hope
He keeps on pointing at the soap
So get on up them stairs
And wash off those dirty layers
And stop acting like a dope

Mum I can't wash
I can't wash myself
Get rid of the dirt
And it will be bad for my health

Remember, get the fruit from between your toes
Swill all the bogies from your nose
Wash all your dangley bits
Scrape the dirt from your arm pits
We might need to use the garden hose!

Mum I can't wash
I can't wash myself
Get rid of the dirt
And it will be bad for my health

If I were you I would rush
Before I go to the kitchen for a brush
I'll scrub from your toes to your chin
I'll remove most of the dirty skin
And use a scouring pad on your mush!

Mum I can wash
I can get myself clean
Put your brush away...
Are my teeth supposed to be green?

What Part of a Chicken is..?

I like eating take away chicken,
We buy it in big buckets.
I've seen their legs, breast, wings,
But where the heck's their nuggets?

Money-bags?

Grandad's got a sore bum,
He's not feeling very well.
I know he tries to hide it,
But I can always tell.

His problem is his money,
He says as he smiles.
He must have a lot,
He says that he has piles!

Where's Your Homework?

Smith! Where's your homework?
The dog ate it, Sir.
Oh, ok do it again then

Poulter! Where's your homework?
It burst into flames, Sir.
Oh, ok do it again then

Rudd! Where's your homework?
It was stolen by aliens, Sir.
Oh, ok do it again then

Rendell! Where's your homework?
Here it is, Sir.
But this is a blank sheet of paper!
It's invisible ink, Sir.
Oh, ok good lad

Sexton! Where's your homework?
I haven't done it, Sir.
Why haven't you done it?
Because I watched TV. Instead, Sir.
Do you expect me to believe
Such a stupid excuse boy?

Boy Called Billy

There once was a boy called Billy
Who one day did something quite silly.
He tried to kill a big bee
While he was having a wee
And got stung on the end of his willy.

Lynne

There were lots of women called Lynne
Who loved to party on gin
They would show their knickers with pride
All the men would run and hide
The sight of their undies was a sin!

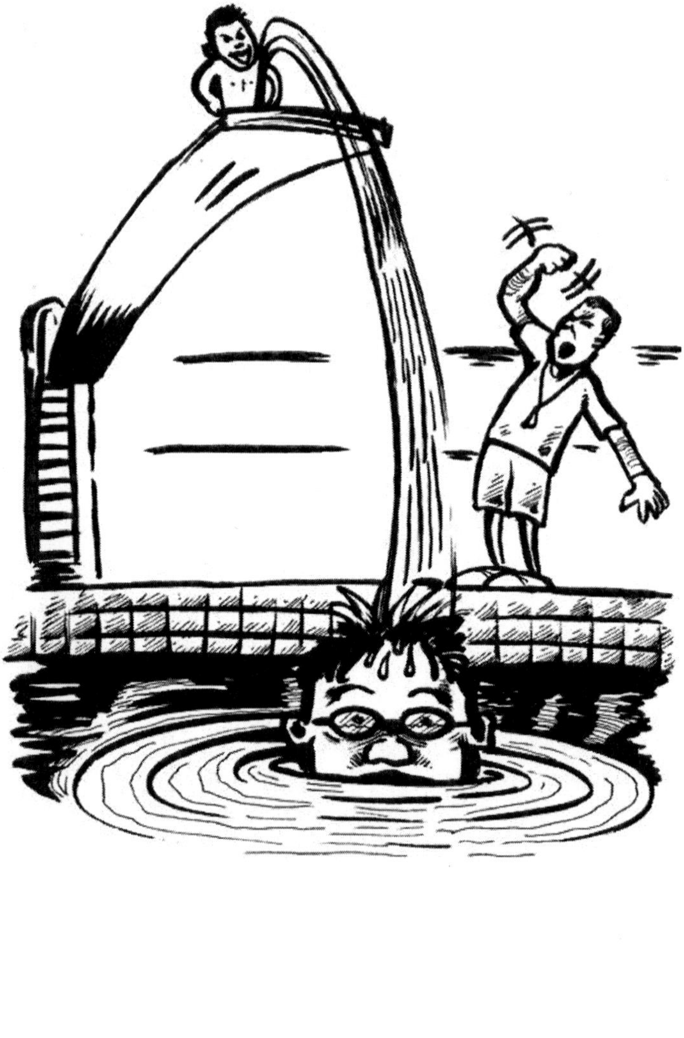

The Swimming Pool

I got kicked out of the swimming baths,
For acting like a fool.
I was standing on the diving board,
And weeing in the pool.
I was such a disgusting child,
The swimming baths man said,
Because I didn't look below me,
And I was weeing on Fred's head.

A Human What?

I must 'ave growed in the garden
Wiv the rest of the greens,
'Cos mi mum has just told mi
That I'm a human bean!

Young Boy From Surrey

There was a young boy from Surrey
Who would eat far too much curry.
He let off a huge fart
Which blew his trousers apart
And covered his room in slurry.

The Price of Love

Mum says that when I grow up
I should marry for love not money,
But she ended up with my dad–
I think she's trying to be funny.

Henry Caterpillar

Little Henry caterpillar
Munching on a leaf
He ate all our vegetables
With his tiny teeth
Soon he'd metamorphosis
And we wouldn't see him again
Dad went and stamped on him
And now he's just a stain!

Ali

There was once a girl called Ali
Who lived in a deep green valley.
To girls, she was bad
This was so sad
Because with boys, she was very pally!

Sharp-Shooting Shirley

Shirley was quite a small dog,
She wouldn't grow much bigger.
They say that she's a gun dog,
But I can't find her trigger!

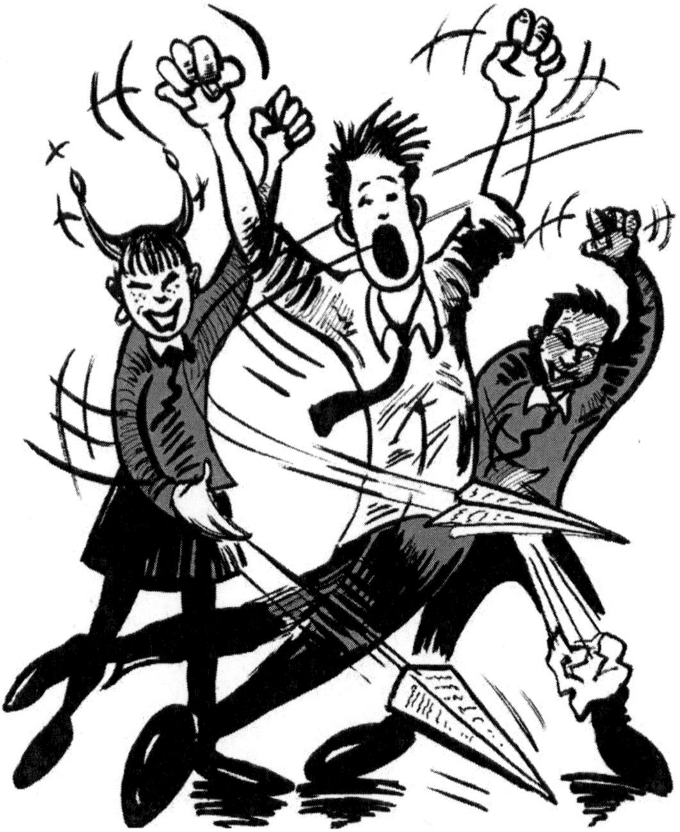

The Class 6 Army Song

I haven't learned a single thing,
Since our poor teacher went missing,
She got herself in such a fix,
Because she had to teach crazy class 6.
She said class 6 have driven her barmy,
So she ran away to join the army,
Now her sergeant major is really rough,
But compared to class 6 he's not that tough.
So, until we get another teacher,
What we're going to say will just not please you.
We'll scream and shout and mess about all day long.

Take A Seat

Jenny had to go to hospital
Which wasn't such a treat–
Someone had squirted superglue
All over the toilet seat

Jenny had sat down
To do what must be done,
But when she sat back up
The seat was stuck to her bum!

A blanket covered poor Jenny,
The whole school let out a cheer,
As she waddled through the playground
With the seat stuck to her rear.

A man then took her details,
He said, "My name's Pete."
He told her not to worry,
Now please, just take a seat."

A nurse took out some pliers,
Jenny let out a scream.
The nurse said, "Don't worry,
They're to open a jar of cream!"

So the seat was removed,
Jenny now knows what to do:
Always check the toilet seat
Before you sit down on the loo!

Get To Bed

I said up inside your bed
Get up inside your bed
I said up inside your bed
Get up inside your bed

Please Mama don't send me up to my room
There's monsters in there, hiding in the gloom
They live off my ear wax and my old toenails
They have razor sharp teeth and big green scales

I said up inside your bed
Get up inside your bed
I said up inside your Bed
Get up inside your bed

Mama they're hiding in my old toy box
They've eaten all my undies and most of my socks
I found one eating the fluff from under my bed
I might wake up in the morning dead.

I said up inside your bed
Get up inside your bed
Up inside your bed
Get up inside your bed

Mama a monster keeps me up all night
He swings up and down on my bedroom light
He wears no trousers and his face is glum
I have to spend all night staring at his bum

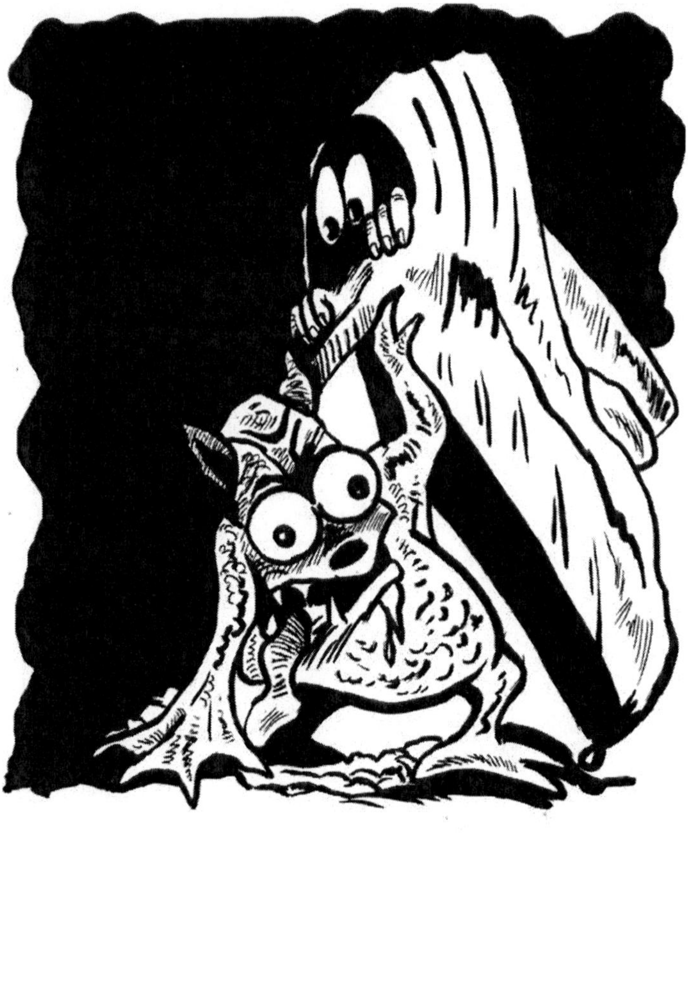

Last time!
Get up inside your bed
Up inside your bed
Get up inside your bed
Up inside your bed

Freddy you have to go up to your room
Santa's on his way and he'll be here soon
And if you're not asleep with your eyes shut tight
Santa won't be leaving you any presents here tonight!
Oop's it's all inside my head
All inside my head
I said oop's inside my head
Now I'm off to bed!

Ferrets

Never put a ferret down your britches
I tried it today
Now I'm in hospital
Having six stitches.

It bit my leg
I was really silly
But it could have been worse,
It could have bit my willy!

How Could You?

I used to have a friend,
Dan was his name.
I no longer see him
Because he's not the same.

He didn't do anything wrong,
It was something that he said.
I couldn't believe my ears,
He must have lost his head!

We were having a conversation
About the way that we feel,
And all the girls we fancy
And if vampires are real.

He then dropped his bombshell,
He wasn't making fun.
He's turned into a weirdo,
He said he fancied my mum!

Ben

There was a young man called Ben
Who would get confused now and then
He just loved to sing
And shake his bling
He wasn't like other men!

There Was A Little Man

There was a little man
Who came from outer space
He had rusty springs for his legs
And whiskers upon his face

He met up with a cat
And said, "How do you do?
I would like to talk with you
Please show me how."

And the cat went.... Gulp, gulp

It was a Cat fish

There was a little man
Who came from outer space
He had rusty springs for his legs
And whiskers upon his face

He met up with a dog
And said, "How do you do?
I would like to talk with you
Please show me how."

And the dog went... Squeak, squeak

It was a Prairie dog

There was a little man
Who came from outer space
He had rusty springs for his legs
And whiskers upon his face

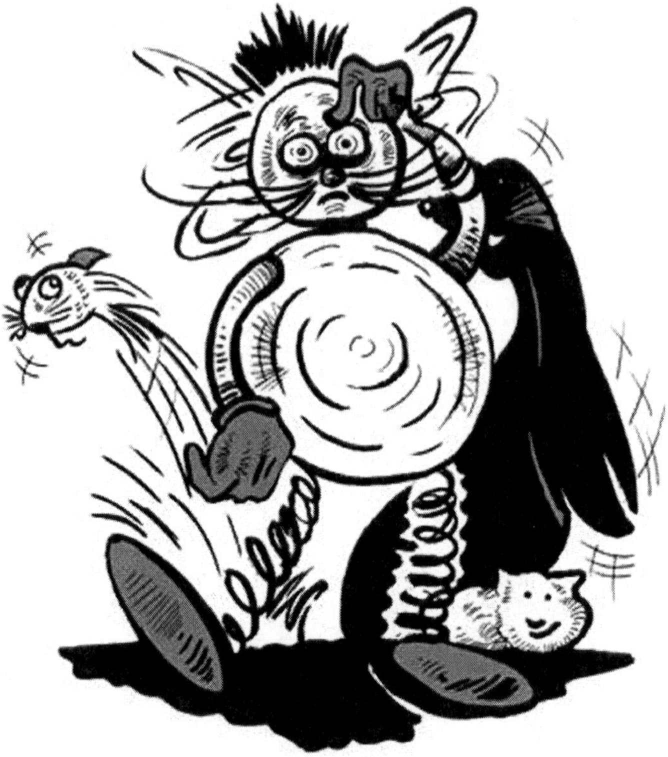

He met up with a pig
And said, "How do you do?
I would like to talk with you
Please show me how."

And the pig went... eek, eek!

It was a Guinea pig

There was a little man
Who came from outer space
He had rusty springs for his legs
And whiskers upon his face

He met up with a lion
And said, "How do you do?
I would like to talk with you
Please show me how."

And the lion went... oink, oink!

It was a Sea lion..

There was a little man
Who came from outer space
He had rusty springs for his legs
And whiskers upon his face

He met up with a cow
And said, "How do you do?
I would like to talk with you
Please show me how."

And the cow said.... simple

He was in Moscow

There was a little man
Who came from outer space
He had rusty springs for his legs
And whiskers upon his face

He met up with a man
And said, "How do you do?
I would like to talk with you
Please show me how."

And the man said.. Guten Tag!

He was a German

There was a little man
who came from outer space
He had met with lots of types
From a cat to a man

But he was sad that human beings
Didn't live inside a can!
He packed up his bags
And left saying what a disgrace

Grandma's Snack

Last Sunday evening
My parents went out for tea.
They invited my Gran round,
Just to sit with me.

I like my Gran,
She's so much fun,
She lets me do things
That would horrify my mum.

So when my parents
Were safely out of the way,
I asked my Gran
"Could I bring my rabbit in to play?

Gran thought for a moment,
Then she said "Yes,
But remember my girl,
You clean up any mess."

So I bought in Floppy,
And put her on the settee.
The first thing she did
Was to have a good pee.

Then she leaped into the air
And ran for the door,
Leaving lots of black droppings
All over the room floor.

So I caught hold of Floppy,
And put her back into her hutch.
I shook my finger at her
Saying, "Well, thanks ever so much."

I sneaked into the kitchen
Where Gran was cooking.
I pinched a paper bag
Very quickly, without stopping.

It was then I had a 'phone call,
So I put the bag on the table,
And I walked into the hall,
As fast as I was able.

It was my friend Jenny;
She'd 'phoned to tell me about her new pups,
But once she started talking
I just couldn't shut her up.

In the end I said,
"Look, Jenny, I really have to go."
So I put down the 'phone,
Then I turned and screamed "OH NO!"

You see, Gran didn't have her glasses,
And without them she cannot see.
And she was eating out of the paper bag,
Saying, "These raisins taste off to me."

Holiday

We went away on holiday
We went to sunny Spain
Mum and Dad ate ecoli
So we won't go there again

We went away on holiday
In a tent way down south
It rained for thirteen days
Followed by an outbreak of foot and mouth!
The rain it caused a flood
We didn't see the sun, not one day
We didn't pack the backup tent
Because it had floated away!

We went away on holiday
To a theme park in the states
Dad was cursing and moaning
As we queued up at the gates
He had become so grumpy
And turned into a total nark
Complaining that for what he'd paid
He could build his own theme park

We went away on holiday
For some culture over in France
But Dad drank too much wine
And asked the tour guide for a dance
The guide she said, "Ze Brithish
Are an utter and total disgrace!"
Mum she lost her temper
And punched her in the face.

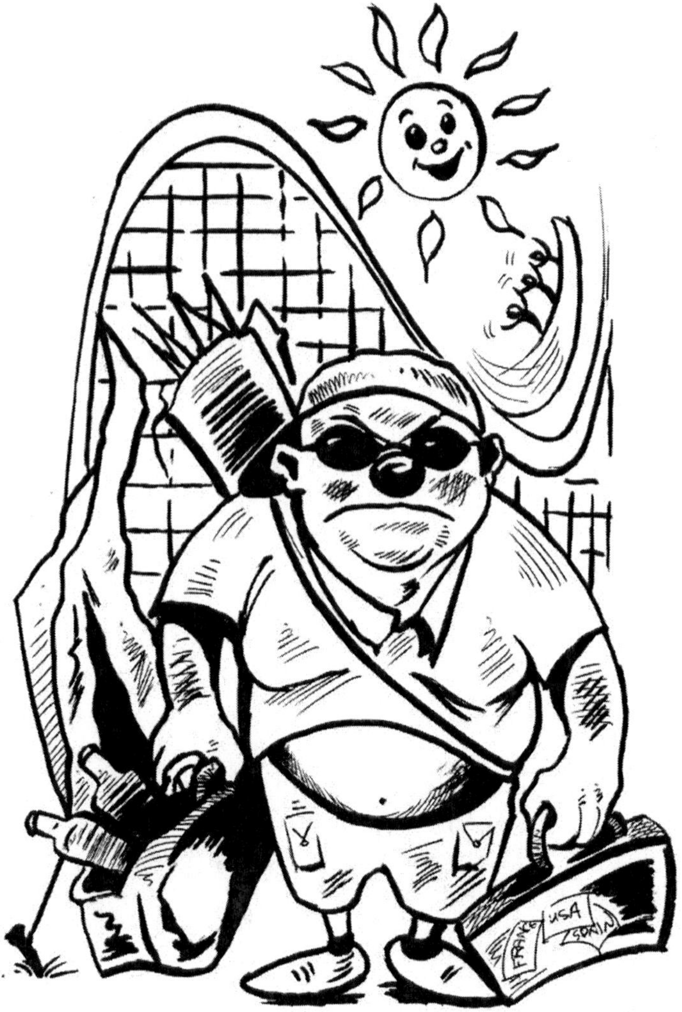
FRANCE
USA
SPAIN

This year we're not going on holiday
We're staying at home for a rest
And the world wide holiday industry
Said they thought it was for the best!?

Acrostic

Slimy nose mucus
Nice and rubbery
Often eaten
Tissues not needed

Funny smelling
A loud roar
Rear end burp
Thunder pants

Bad breath
Unusual smell
Repeating food
Passion killer

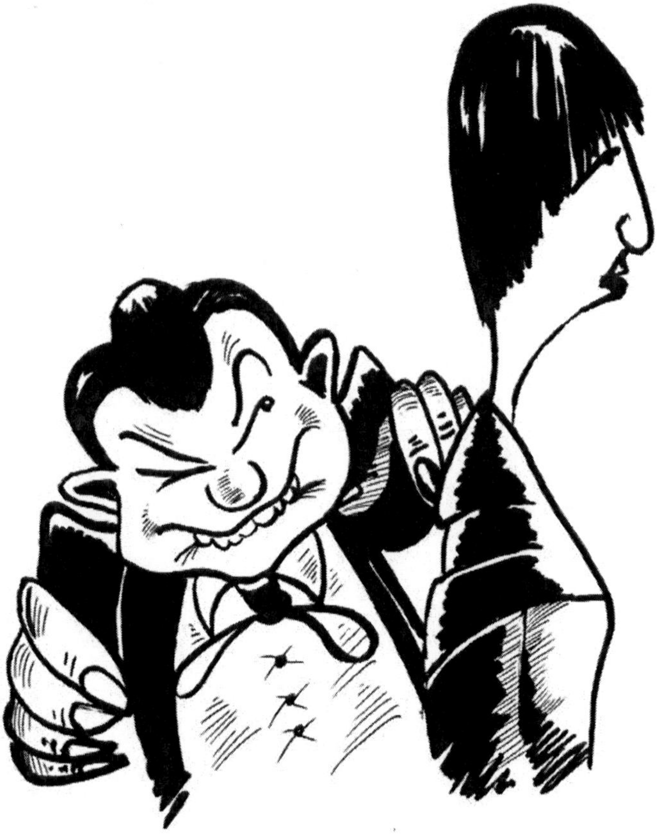

Vampires

My girlfriend she loves vampires
She thinks they're really ace
So I bit her on the neck
And she hit me in the face!

The Lumpy Bird

How absurd, the lumpy bird.
If you make him jump,
He turns into a lump,
And lies on the floor
Like a turd.

The Prayer Of A Bad Boy

Every night I go to sleep
I pray my new teacher's not a creep.
I hope my old teacher doesn't come back
Or ever find out that I got her the sack.

I pray my pet snake will be found soon
After escaping in my mum's bedroom.
I pray my sister doesn't have a rage
Because I opened the door on her hamster's cage.

I pray that my mum doesn't feel any stress
When she sees the kite made from her new dress.
I hope that Grandad has a sense of humour
When he finds his false teeth stuck up the Hoover.

And so I end my nightly prayer:
Make my Headmaster work elsewhere.
Please watch over me, I think you should,
Because just of late I've been quite good.

Louise

There was once a young girl called Louise
Who was very hard to please
She hatched a cunning plan
To get a new man
She prayed every night on her knees!

Jeff

There was once a young man called Jeff
Who would scare the girls half to death
He was so very nice
But he had head lice
And very, very bad breath!

Barry

There was once a young man called Barry
Who had a big bag he would carry
The bag he would hide
So no one saw inside
He's not the type you would marry!

Teacher

I think my new teacher is mad
Her behaviour was very bad
What do you think
Of a woman who likes to drink
Then tries to snog your Dad!

The Classic Dancer

I will tell you a story,
But I will tell it in rhyme,
It's about a party,
And having a good time.

It was grandma's party,
She was ninety years old,
She was sipping sherry
Like a merry old soul.
The music was playing,
It was very loud,
When I noticed a dancer
In the middle of a crowd.

He was just stood there
With his arms in the air,
Waddling his bum
Like he hadn't a care.
He flapped his arms,
Just like a chicken,
He bobbed his head,
Then started clucking.
Cluck, cluck, cluck cluck cluck.

I said, "Look here mum,
Look at this man.
Get over here,
As fast as you can."

We started laughing,
Saying he must be mad.
Then we let out a scream
When we realised it was dad.

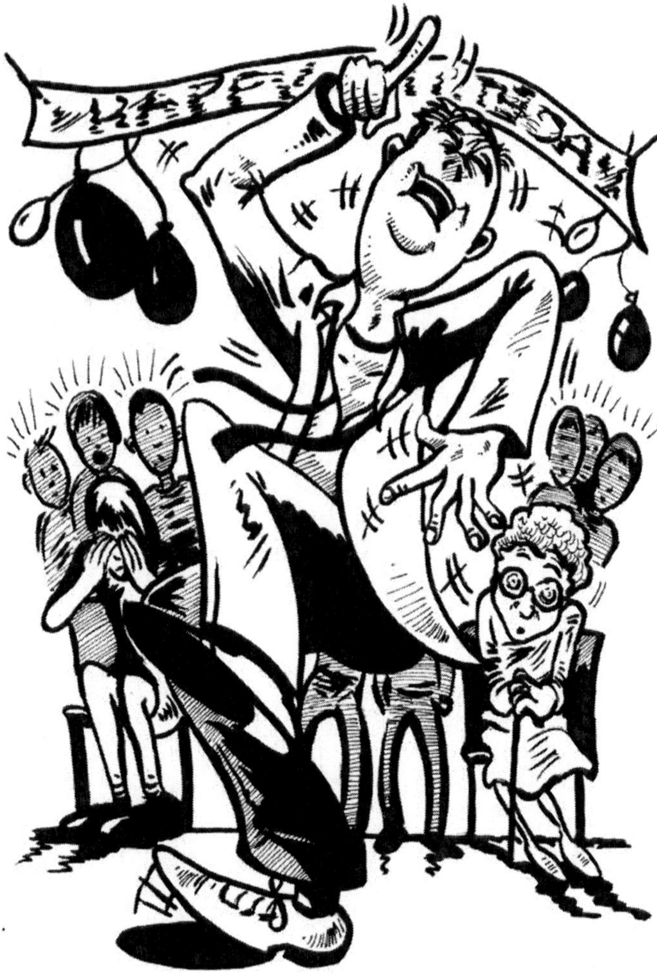

He was just stood there,
With his arms in the air,
Waddling his bum
Like he hadn't a care.
He flapped his arms,
Just like a chicken
He bobbed his head
Then started clucking.
Cluck, cluck, cluck cluck cluck.

The music was loud,
Our ears were ringing.
There was worse to come,
Dad started singing.

He was telling people
He was Baby Spice,
You have never seen
Such a sight in your life.

He was just stood there,
With his arms in the air,
Waddling his bum
Like he hadn't a care.
He flapped his arms,
Just like a chicken
He bobbed his head
Then started clucking.
Cluck, cluck, cluck cluck cluck.

Then dad grabbed granny,
And swung her round.
Her teeth fell out,
Landing on the ground.

Mum gave dad
Such a smack
Saying, "Stupid fool,
She'll have a heart attack."

People were laughing,
It was so embarrassing,
But not for dad.

He just kept on dancing. He was just stood there,
With his arms in the air,
Waddling his bum
Like he hadn't a care.
He flapped his arms,
Just like a chicken
He bobbed his head
Then started clucking.
Cluck, cluck, cluck cluck cluck.

Poor old dad
Was losing pace,
His shirt wide open,
Sweat on his face.

His dancing's caused
By a drinking binge.
The stupid lump
Just made me cringe.

So if you think
That alcohol is cool,
Remember my dad,
That could be YOU!

Just stood there,
With your arms in the air,
Waddling your bum

Like you hadn't a care.
Flapping your arms,
Just like a chicken
Bobbing your head
Then starting clucking.
Cluck, cluck, cluck cluck cluck.

People were laughing
It was so embarrassing,
But not for dad,
He just kept on dancing.

Moths

Moths are attracted to light bulbs,
They bang their heads on them until they fall.
Dad says he's attracted to women,
And that's like banging your head against a wall!

Stinky Teachers

Why do teachers
Have bad breath
That to small children
Could cause death
At twenty yards
If I'm not wrong?
A deadly gasp,
A lethal pong.
The reason is
Late at night
Teachers are found,
What a sorry sight,
In your dustbins
Looking for food;
Mouldy old curries
Get them in the mood.
It's all washed down
With maggot soup
Which gives them wind,
It makes them poop.
So if your teacher
Breathes on you
This is what you must do:
Don't breathe in,
Give them a hint–
Turn the other way
Then offer a mint.

The Nativity

Ladies and gentlemen
Welcome here today
To watch our Nativity
And watch the children play

Kevin is playing Joseph
He's a creepy little swine
Miss Davis gave him the part
When it really should be mine

And Chloe's playing Mary
Ickle baby cheeses Muver
Ah, Chloe is so ugly
She'd be better playing his bruvver

And then we have the three wise men
Riding upon their mount
Well one can't tie his laces up
And the other two can't count

Oh yes, then we have the shepherds
Who watch their flocks at night
Well two of them would wet themselves
If you just turn out the light!

Then we have ickle baby cheeses
Just laying in his manger
Well he's just a plastic doll
That was a power ranger!

And then we have the chorus
Skipping from the wing
These are just all the kids
That can't dance or act or sing

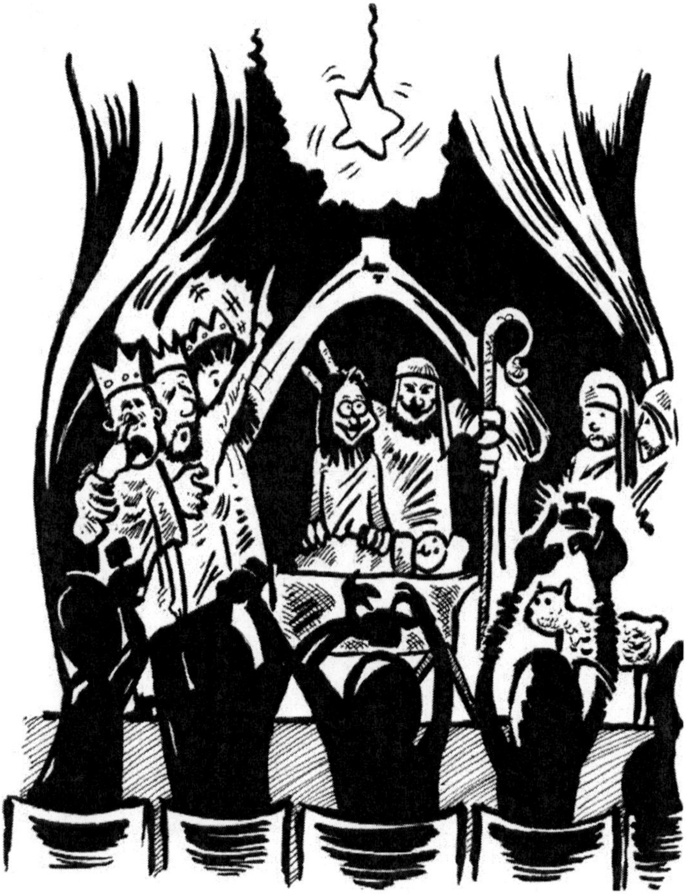

Then we have me...
The Nativity narrator
Next time give me Joseph
And you lot.. See you later!

Mr............

I think my teacher's a fool
I wish he didn't teach at my school.
He shouts and he rants,
Wears green flared pants,
And thinks mathematics is cool.

The Graveyard

This poem should be told to your friend in a low eerie voice. When you get to the last word, "You", shout it out and watch them jump out of their skins.

The wind was howling,
I was all alone.
It was late at night,
I couldn't find my way home.
I came to the graveyard,
I opened the gate.
My heart beat with such a rate.
As I walked among the grey headstones
I felt like crying,
I wanted to go home.
It was then that I heard it,
It was a ghostly sort of voice.
The chill of the wind
Made it an even more eerie noise.
The voice said,
"Are you scared?"
I stuttered, "W-w-who?"
Then there was silence,
And the voice said

"YOU!"

The French Toilet

While on holiday
With my family in France,
I met a man,
Just by chance.
I was looking for the toilets,
I was by myself,
But I couldn't read the signs,
I needed some help.
I asked this man,
"Is this toilet for me?"
He nodded his head,
Then he said "Oui."
I said, "No I don't,
I want to pooh,
And I think you're so rude,
So what's it to you?

The Phoenix

The phoenix was a mythical bird
That could never be burned;
It rose out of a fire
And lots of fame it earned.

But it's not as good as a chicken,
No matter how good it looked
Because you could never eat it,
There's no way it could be cooked.

Perfect Recipe

To get the perfect curry,
I have some advice for you.
If you have a pen ready,
This is what I do.
First I get together some money,
Then I look up my favourite recipe.
Then I phone up the local curry house,
And they deliver it to me!

Old Ted

Mum wants me to throw away
My faithful old Ted,
But my life wouldn't be the same
Without his cuddles in bed.

We've been through a lot,
Old Teddy and me,
We've chased away monsters
That only we can see.

The time mum got angry
Sending me to my room,
Teddy stood by me
In my hours of gloom.

And when I was poorly
I gave off a strange smell;
No one would come near me
But Teddy stayed until I was well.

So I couldn't ask him to leave
And vacate my bed;
Besides, I've hidden some money
In the back of his head.

Todd and Rod

There was once a boy called Todd,
Who had a good friend called Rod.
They would walk through the sands
Holding each other's hands–
I always thought they were odd.

Young Girl Called Liz

There was once a young girl called Liz,
Who thought she was such a whiz,
But she was a right Herbert,
She ate too much sherbet,
Causing her wee-wee to fizz

The Snigger

One cold autumn's morning
A lovely young lass
Wore a pair of new green tights
To her new school class

She thought they were fine
She thought they were cool
She wore them with pride
To her new school

But as she entered the room
The noise fell to a hush
They stared at the girl
Who then started to blush

They muttered a while
'It's the worst they had seen'
They all wore black tights
And hers were well.. green!

It was then that it happened
A very small snigger
But like all bits of hate
It would soon get bigger

The snigger it grew
And turned into a jeer
The girl was frightened
And gripped with fear

Then came the pointing
And calling of names
Which started the pushing
And playing of games

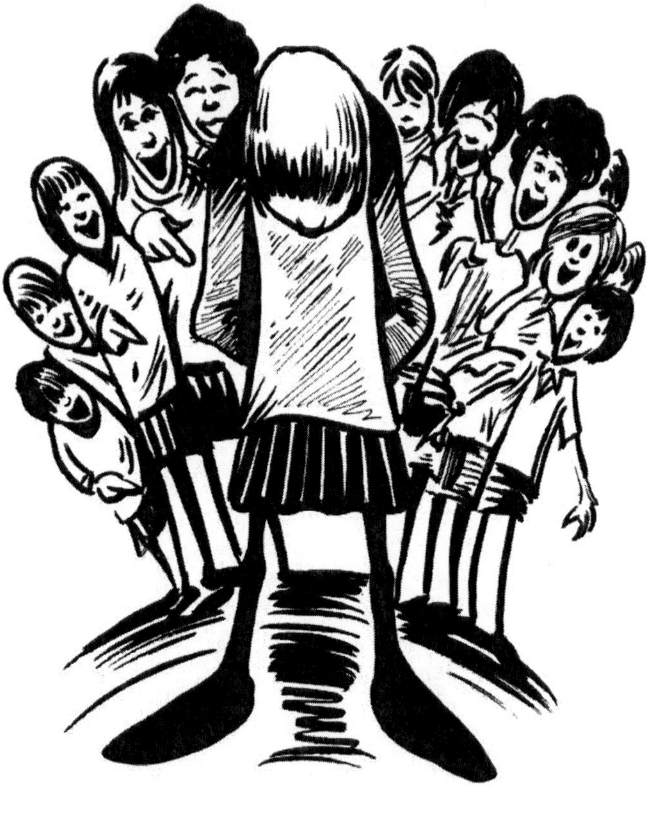

They surrounded the girl
They all wanted their fights
Just because a young girl
Dare to wear green tights

The girl ran from the room
To the sound of loud cheers
Her heart filled with pain,
Her eyes filled with tears

Her confidence now broken
She took to her bed
Refusing to get up
No matter what was said

Time had now passed
Since that awful day
The girl hadn't returned
She was hidden away

Soon all the girls
Talked of an event so big
A super star singer
Would perform, a one off gig

What would she wear
It would certainly be cool
And be copied the next day
By the girls at the school

So came the night
Of which everyone had talked
The music was loud
On stage the superstar walked

The girls they all gasped
Through the smoke and the lights
Because up on the stage
Was a super star wearing .. Green tights

Well the girls couldn't believe it
They knew it was so cool
On Monday to wear black tights
Would make you look a fool

So the very next day
All over the land
Girls ran to the shops
With money in hand

From the north to the south
Not one girl would be seen
Wearing any other colour
They only wore green

The girl she sat
In her room all alone
No friends to talk to
No one to phone

But it all became clear
When she saw on TV
What girls were wearing
"They're all following me!"

It's the latest fashion craze
Where all girls must be seen
Black tights are out
Cool girls must wear green

So with those words
Like being awoken from a sleep
She realised she was a leader
Not one of the sheep

It's good to be different
And fashion is so hollow
She would dress as she liked,
And let others would follow

So she threw back her bed sheets
And jumped from her bed
She was going back to school
And her tights shall be.. RED!

We're Finished (His Story)

It was on the cards,
It had to happen.
You always pestered me,
You wouldn't stop yapping.
You hated my friends,
You hated my sports.
You hated my clothes,
Even hated my shorts.
Nothing can please you,
You were never happy.
The last time you laughed
You'd poohed in your nappy!

We're Finished (Her Story)

Too right it's over,
It could never work.
It was so difficult
Spending time with a jerk.
You loved your mates,
You loved your sports.
You looked such a plonker
In those stupid shorts.
For you I'm not right,
I'm bad for your health.
You don't need my love,
You're in love with yourself!

Late One Night

It was late one night,
I was going to sleep.
The house was silent,
Not as much as a peep.
When through the gloom
Of my bedroom
Came a terrible voice,
The voice of doom.
So I did what you do,
When you are laid in bed,
And something scares you,
I pulled the covers over my head!
"My name is Dracula".
Said the scary voice,
Well I weed a little,
And not by choice.
"Come over here my dear,
And let me see your face."
I replied, "I'd rather not."
My heart was pumping at a pace!
Then I heard music,
I thought, 'that's not right?
Dracula doesn't take an orchestra,
To give people a fright!"
So I peered from under the covers,
And I thought silly me!
It wasn't a visit from the un-dead,
But a film on my TV!